BRITISH RAILWAYS STEAMING THROUGH THE FIFTIES

Volume Three

Compiled by
PETER HANDS & COLIN RICHARDS

DEFIANT PUBLICATIONS
190 Yoxall Road
Shirley, Solihull
West Midlands

Printed in the United Kingdom by Netherwood Dalton & Co Ltd, Huddersfield, England

CURRENT STEAM PHOTOGRAPH ALBUMS AVAILABLE FROM DEFIANT PUBLICATIONS–

British Railways Steaming through The Sixties

VOLUME 1
OUT OF PRINT

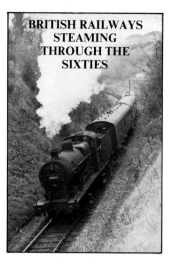

VOLUME 2
A4 size - Softback. 100 pages
- 182 b/w photographs.
£5.95 + 60p postage.
ISBN 0 946857 01 6.

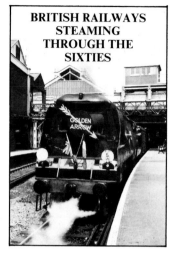

VOLUME 3
A4 size - Hardback. 100 pages
- 182 b/w photographs.
£7.95 + 75p postage.
ISBN 0 946857 02 4.

VOLUME 4
A4 size - Hardback. 100 pages
- 182 b/w photographs.
£7.95 + 75p postage.
ISBN 0 946857 04 0.

VOLUME 5
A4 size - Hardback. 100 pages
- 180 b/w photographs.
£7.95 + 75p postage.
ISBN 0 946857 06 7.

VOLUME 6
A4 size - Hardback. 100 pages
- 182 b/w photographs.
£8.45 + 75p postage.
ISBN 0 946857 08 3.

VOLUME 7
A4 size - Hardback. 100 pages
- 182 b/w photographs.
£8.45 + 75p postage.
ISBN 0 946857 10 5.

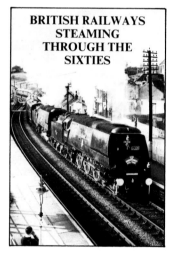

VOLUME 8
A4 size - Hardback. 100 pages
- 181 b/w photographs.
£8.95 + 75p postage.
ISBN 0 946857 14 8.

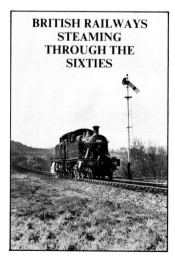

VOLUME 9
IN
PREPARATION
JULY 1988

BRITISH RAILWAYS STEAMING THROUGH THE SIXTIES

IN
PREPARATION

VOLUME 10

BRITISH RAILWAYS STEAMING THROUGH THE SIXTIES

IN
PREPARATION

VOLUME 11

BRITISH RAILWAYS STEAMING THROUGH THE SIXTIES

IN
PREPARATION

VOLUME 12

Individual Regional Albums

VOLUME 1
A4 size - Hardback. 100 pages
- 188 b/w photographs.
£7.95 + 75p postage.
ISBN 0 946857 03 2.

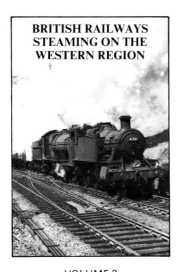

VOLUME 2
A4 size - Hardback. 100 pages
- 181 b/w photographs.
£8.45 + 75p postage.
ISBN 0 946857 11 03.

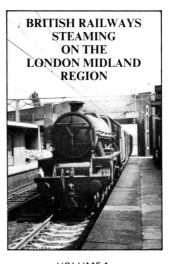

VOLUME 1
A4 size - Hardback. 100 pages
- 184 b/w photographs.
£7.95 + 75p postage.
ISBN 0 946857 05 9.

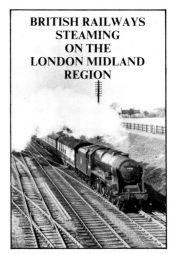

VOLUME 2
A4 size - Hardback. 100 pages
- 181 b/w photographs.
£8.95 + 75p postage.
ISBN 0 946857 15 6.

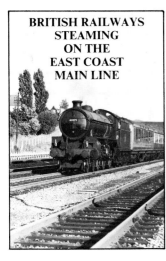

A4 size - Hardback. 100 pages
- 183 b/w photographs.
£7.95 + 75p postage.
ISBN 0 946857 07 5.

VOLUME 1
IN
PREPARATION
JULY 1988

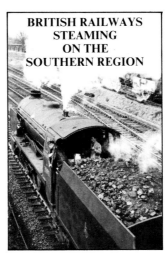

VOLUME 1
A4 size - Hardback. 100 pages
- 188 b/w photographs.
£8.45 + 75p postage.
ISBN 0 946857 09 1.

BRITISH RAILWAYS STEAMING ON THE SOUTHERN REGION

IN
PREPARATION

VOLUME 2

VOLUME 1
A4 size - Hardback. 100 pages
-180 b/w photographs.
£8.95 + 75p postage.
ISBN 0 946857 12 1.

VOLUME 2
A4 size - Hardback. 100 pages
-180 b/w photographs.
£8.95 + 75p postage.
ISBN 0 946857 13 X.

VOLUME 3
A4 size - Hardback. 100 pages
-180 b/w photographs.
£9.95 + 75p postage.
ISBN 0 946857 16 4

VOLUME 4
A4 size - Hardback. 100 pages
-180 b/w photographs.
£9.95 + 75p postage.
ISBN 0 946857 17 2

OTHER TITLES AVAILABLE FROM DEFIANT PUBLICATIONS
PRICES VARY FROM £1 to £3.80 INCLUDING POSTAGE

WHAT HAPPENED TO STEAM

This series of booklets, 50 in all, is designed to inform the reader of the allocations, re-allocations and dates of withdrawal of steam locomotives during their last years of service. From 1957 onwards and finally where the locomotives concerned were stored and subsequently scrapped.

BR STEAM SHED ALLOCATIONS

This series lists all individual steam locomotives based at the different parent depots of B.R. from January 1957 until each depot either closed to steam or closed completely. All regions have been completed with the exception of the London Midland which will be dealt with during 1987.

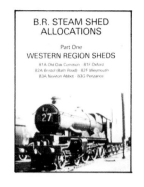

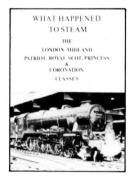

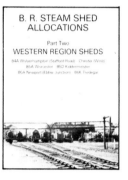
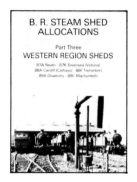

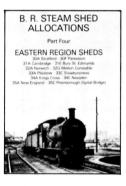
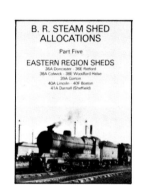

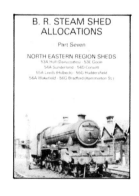

CHASING STEAM ON SHED

PETER HANDS

BARBRYN PRESS £5.95 + 50p POSTAGE

ISBN 0 906160 030

This is an account of a locospotters life during the years of 1956-1968. In 1956 when there were 18 000 or so steam locomotives on B.R. it was every locospotters ambition to set eyes on as many locomotives as possible, especially before they were withdrawn.

Every trainspotter will remember "shed bashing" trips, some official, mostly unofficial, the challenge they represented and the feeling of delight of having achieved of what was regarded in some cases as the impossible. All these are relived with an almost uncanny accurateness.

We also plot through the various exploits of other railway trips of which there are many positively hilarious accounts and these are backed up most commendably by a series of cartoon illustrations which often capture the mood and atmosphere of those days so perfectly.

Depending on your age, this book will either bring back lots of memories, make you realise what you missed or if you were too young to participate will let you realise what good days they were.

....

Lineside Camera Series by G. W. Sharpe.

	8″ × 8″ Approx
East Coast Pacifics	48 Pages £1.95 + 30p postage.
Yorkshire Steam	48 Pages £1.95 + 30p postage.
Pennine Steam	48 Pages £1.95 + 30p postage.
BR Standard Steam	36 Pages £2.25 + 30p postage.
Diesels in the Sixties	36 Pages £2.25 + 30p postage.
Named Express	36 Pages £2.25 + 30p postage.
Western Express Steam	36 Pages £2.50 + 30p postage.

ACKNOWLEDGEMENTS

Grateful thanks are extended to the following contributors of photographs not only for their use in this book but for their kind patience and long term loan of negatives/ photographs whilst this book was being compiled.

K. BARROW
BLETCHLEY

H. H. BLEADS
BIRMINGHAM

B. W. L. BROOKSBANK
LONDON

N. L. BROWNE
ALDERSHOT

L. BROWNHILL
BRIERLEY HILL

R. S. CARPENTER
BIRMINGHAM

BRIAN COATES
AYLESFORD

E. A. ELIAS
WOLVERHAMPTON

A. N. H. GLOVER
BIRMINGHAM

J. D. GOMERSALL
SHEFFIELD

B. K. B. GREEN
BRAMHALL

PETER HAY
HOVE

J. HEAD
TENTERDEN

R. W. HINTON
GLOUCESTER

F. HORNBY
NORTH CHEAM

A. C. INGRAM
WISBECH

L. C. JACKS
BIRMINGHAM

D. K. JONES
MOUNTAIN ASH

M. JOYCE
HITCHIN

TERRY NICHOLLS
BRISTOL

J. D. OWENS
STOCKPORT

W. POTTER
BISHOPS CLEEVE

N. E. PREEDY
HUCCLECOTE

G. W. SHARPE
BARNSLEY

M. S. STOKES
MARPLE

A. WAKEFIELD
DRONFIELD

G. H. WILSON
BIRMINGHAM

G. WOOD
BIRMINGHAM

Front Cover — Former Midland Railway Class 4F 0-6-0 No 43871 is a long way from its home shed of 55B Stourton as it hauls a goods train consisting of hopper wagons through Grange-over-Sands in 1957. (A. C. Ingram)

ISBN 0 946857 16 4

©P. B. HANDS/C. RICHARDS 1988
FIRST PUBLISHED 1988

INTRODUCTION

BRITISH RAILWAYS STEAMING THROUGH THE FIFTIES – Volume Three was scheduled to be published in July 1988 along with Volume Four. With the popular demand for these 1950's albums it was decided to bring the publication date back to March 1988. The authors hope the reader will enjoy the diverse variety of locomotives and locations within the pages of these albums.

The 'BR Steaming' books are designed to give the ordinary, everyday steam photographic enthusiast of the 1950's and 1960's a chance to participate in and give pleasure to others whilst recapturing the twilight days of steam.

Apart from the 1950's and 1960's series, individual regional albums will be produced from time to time. Wherever possible no famous names will be found but the content and quality of the majority of photographs will be second to none.

In many respects the 1950's represented the most enjoyable period for post-war steam enthusiasts. Thousands of steam locomotives abounded from Wick to Penzance and with the construction of BR Standard locomotives, the future for steam looked secure for many years to come. The general cleanliness of steam engines in the 1950's was far superior to the 1960's, as was the large variety of classes still in general service. Who would have envisaged by 1958, with only small numbers of diesels in service, that within a decade steam would be finished.

BRITISH RAILWAYS STEAMING THROUGH THE FIFTIES – Volume Three is divided into nine chapters encompassing England, Scotland and Wales. Though appearing on the surface to be strictly regionalised, in many cases i.e. The London area, The South-West and Wales contain photographs from a mixture of regions.

It was also a difficult task to differentiate where borders start and finish, e.g. the dividing line between the London area and the chapters concerning the Eastern and Southern Regions. Similar problems occur on deciding the dividing lines between the Southern Region, The South-West, The Midlands and the North-West. The authors hopefully have managed to create an enjoyable balance between these *grey* areas.

The continuation of the 'BR Steaming' series etc., depends upon you the reader. If you feel you have suitable material of BR steam locomotives between 1948-1968 and wish to contribute them towards the series and other future publications please contact either:

Peter Hands,
190 Yoxall Road,
Shirley, Solihull,
West Midlands B90 3RN

OR

Colin Richards
28 Kendrick Close,
Damson Parkway, Solihull,
West Midlands B92 0QD

CONTENTS

NAMEPLATES — Example nameplates from the four main companies which represented British Railways.

1) GWR *Grange* Class 4-6-0 No 6813 *Eastbury Grange*. (N. E. Preedy)

2) SR N15X Class 4-6-0 No 32333 *Remembrance*. (Peter Hay)

3) LMS *Jubilee* Class 4-6-0 No 45721 *Impregnable*. (A. Wakefield)

4) LNER B17/1 Class 4-6-0 No 61640 *Somerleyton Hall*. (Peter Hay)

CHAPTER ONE — LONDON AREA

5)   Steam sizzling from the safety valves is proof enough that the fireman's early preparations can enable him to take it easy as he looks towards the camera as his charge accelerates out of the magnificent terminus of Paddington on the Western Region. The locomotive concerned is GWR *Castle* Class 4-6-0 No 5052 *Earl of Radnor* on a down express duty in the summer of 1954. (G. W. Sharpe)

6) Stanier LMS Class 4 2-6-4T No 42088 passes under a smoke-blackened road bridge and nears Upper Warlingham on the southern fringes of London with a three coach local passenger train in May 1952. Upper Warlingham once belonged to the Croydon and Oxted Joint Railway (LBSC & SEC), a grandiose title if ever there was one. (G. W. Sharpe)

7) A rake of elderly suburban coaches hauled by LNER N7 Class 0-6-2T No 69670 (30A Stratford) arrives at Enfield Town from Liverpool Street on 20th September 1958. In the left of the picture is sister engine No 69663, also based at Stratford, shunting empty stock. Note the interesting signal gantry in the foreground complete with indicator panels. (F. Hornby)

8)   An ex. South East & Chatham Railway E1 Class 4-4-0 No 31497 in spotless external condition blows off a nice head of steam outside the straight shed at its home depot of Bricklayers Arms on 14th April 1957. Alongside 31497 is sister engine No 31504, a visitor from 73A Stewarts Lane. (J. D. Gomersall)

9)   Evening sunlight casts a mighty shadow over the station at Watford Junction on 26th June 1954. A crew member relaxes on a bench on the platform with only a gentle hiss of steam from the safety valves of BR Class 4 2-6-4T No 80037 to disturb him. No doubt, his few moments of peace will soon be over and he will be heading southwards with his charge. (K. Barrow)

10) LNER A3 Class 4-6-2 No 60044 *Melton* (34A Kings Cross) is admired by a smattering of onlookers after backing on to its train, the 3.10 pm to Newcastle at Kings Cross station on 15th July 1958. The driver looks out of the cab as his fireman (complete with cigarette dangling from his lips) walks to the front of the locomotive with a lamp. (M. Joyce)

11) As one heads westwards from Paddington the first depot after Old Oak Common is at 81B Slough, a small four road straight shed which was used mainly to supply locomotives for suburban, freight and shunting duties. Photographed in front of the shed on 10th August 1957 is GWR 5700 Class 0-6-0PT No 4638 taking a week-end breather from its normal roles. (J. D. Gomersall)

12) In steam days especially in the major cities, depots were often to be found within a short distance of each other. Kings Cross on the Eastern Region had its own shed and only four miles away from Kings Cross station was another depot at 34B Hornsey where LNER N2 Class 0-6-2T No 69501 is photographed on 22nd September 1957. (N. E. Preedy)

13) The graceful lines of a GWR 'Dukedog' Class 4-4-0 No 9023 from 82C Swindon, in pristine condition are scarcely noticed by the public at the far end of Victoria station on the Southern Region on 25th April 1954. 9023, on this occasion, is about to participate on a Railway Correspondence and Travel Society railtour. (N. L. Browne)

14) Overlooked by massive gasometers, a Derby based LMS *Jubilee* Class 4-6-0 No 45585 *Hyderabad* waits to depart light engine from St. Pancras after bringing in an up express on 31st March 1956. The grubby, filthy and generally unkempt condition of *Hyderabad* was the exception rather than the norm in the 1950's but the 1960's would soon reverse this situation. (N. L. Browne)

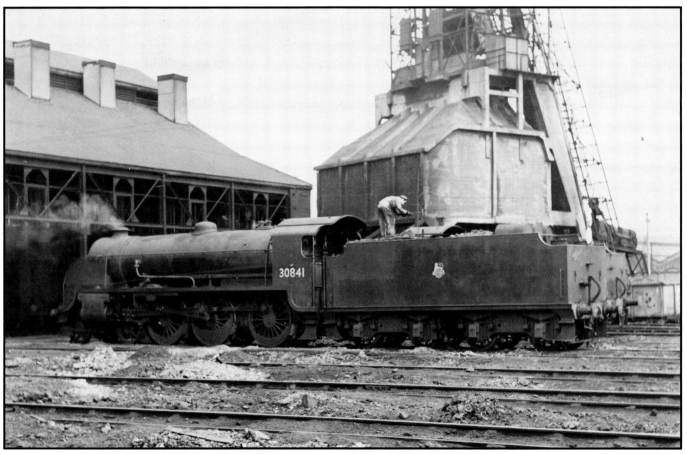

15) The huge concrete coaling plant at 70A Nine Elms dwarfs the clean lines of SR S15 Class 4-6-0 No 30841 as it is prepared for the road in the apparently almost deserted yard of the shed on 8th August 1957. 30841 is a rather unusual visitor being based at 72A Exmouth Junction on the outskirts of Exeter. (J. D. Gomersall)

16) Having transgressed beyond the board pronouncing 'no engine to pass this board' an immaculate LNER D16 Class 4-4-0 No 62567 from 31A Cambridge awaits departure from Bishopsgate Goods station with an RCTS railtour bound for East Anglia on 6th September 1953. Bishopsgate was the first GER London terminal station. (Peter Hay)

17) The Hawksworth *County* Class 4-6-0's were the last passenger locomotive design to emerge from the GWR stable, being introduced in 1945. One of the 83D Laira (Plymouth) batch No 1015 *County of Gloucester* simmers in the yard at 81A Old Oak Common shed on 15th March 1959. *County of Gloucester* was equipped with a double chimney in November 1958. (N. E. Preedy)

18) The crew of ex. North London Railway, later LMS Class 2F 0-6-0T No 58857 pose for a special 'photo-call' in bright sunshine in the shed yard at 1D Devons Road Bow on 14th April 1957. This depot was located on the east side of the Bow to Poplar line to the south of Bow station (NLR) which had closed in 1945. The days of these North London tanks were also numbered, 58857 being withdrawn in April 1958. (J. D. Gomersall)

19) For a brief period of time Liverpool Street station was provided with a small selection of 'bulled up' station pilots. To cope with the heavier trains was a lined out and polished LNER N7 Class 0-6-2T No 69614 based at the nearby shed of 30A Stratford and is seen at Liverpool Street on 13th April 1957 awaiting its next turn of duty. (J. D. Gomersall)

20) The absurd stovepipe chimney does nothing to enhance the appearance of the massive SR H16 Class 6F 4-6-2T No 30520 as it approaches the camera at Vauxhall on a murky January day in 1950 at the head of a lengthy empty stock train. 30520 is carrying the logo of its new owners on its side tanks. (G. W. Sharpe)

21) The clean lines and parallel boiler of the Thompson LNER B1 Class 4-6-0's are shown off to perfection in this superb study of No 61008 *Kudo* seen at rest in the yard of its home shed at 30A Stratford on 20th April 1952. Stratford, in its hey-day, was the largest depot on British Railways, finally closing its doors to steam in September 1962. (N. E. Preedy)

22) Ex. London, Tilbury & Southend Railway Class 3F 0-6-0T No 41980 waits for the shed driver before moving into the depot at 33A Plaistow on 14th April 1957. By this date in time Plaistow shed was starting to look run down, housing a motley collection of engines. It lost its code in November 1959 becoming a sub-shed of Tilbury and closed completely in June 1962. (J. D. Gomersall)

23) Situated on the western extremes of London on the Western Region is the delightful town of Maidenhead situated between Slough and Reading. The fireman of Slough based GWR 5700 Class 0-6-0PT No 3697 'poses' for the camera as the locomotive takes refreshment on 26th March 1959. From the way the angle of the camera is, it looks as if the hose from the water column is in the chimney of 3697. (A. C. Ingram)

CHAPTER TWO — SOUTHERN REGION

24) A SR Unrebuilt *Battle of Britain* Class 4-6-2 No 34086 *219 Squadron* speeds past a row of open wagons and a cattle market, in a flurry of white and black smoke at Ashford, at the head of a down boat train destined for London in March 1958. *219 Squadron* allocated to 73A Stewarts Lane was to remain in unrebuilt form until withdrawn from Eastleigh in June 1966. (Brian Coates)

25) Looking like a badly designed meccano set on wheels, SR Bulleid 1942 designed 'Austerity' Q1 Class 5F 0-6-0 No 33013 from 70B Feltham is noted at Basingstoke on 22nd August 1959 on the 11.25 am Woking to Salisbury passenger train. These locomotives were to be seen on a number of occasions on this particular train during this period of time. (F. Hornby)

26) The fireman of SR *Schools* Class 4-4-0 No 30927 *Clifton* enjoys the warm summer sunshine blazing on to the footplate on 3rd August 1952. *Clifton* is far from its home shed of Bricklayers Arms, London at the head of a relief express at Folkestone Junction. Transferred to Feltham in January 1961, *Clifton* ended its days at Nine Elms being taken out of service in January 1962. (N. E. Preedy)

27) A member of the diminutive SR B4 Class 0-4-0 Tanks is captured on film on an idyllic July day in 1953 on duty in the heart of the dockland at Dover in between shunting duties. Although the majority of the members of this class were withdrawn by October 1959, three examples Nos 30089, 30096 and 30102 were to survive in service well into 1963. (G. W. Sharpe)

28) Photographed from the lengthy down platform at Bournemouth (Central) in July 1951 is one of the powerful SR *Lord Nelson* Class 4-6-0's No 30864 *Sir Martin Frobisher*, at rest in the shed yard at Bournemouth motive power depot. From this vantage point all of the comings and goings of locomotives to and from the shed could easily be observed. (G. W. Sharpe)

29) Faversham shed yard is the setting for this splendid side-shot of SR D1 Class 4-4-0 No 31509 seen here in light steam on 4th June 1951. The D1 Class were rebuilds by Maunsell of the earlier designed Wainwright locomotives of the D Class and were to be made extinct in February 1962. Faversham depot, coded 73E, closed in June 1959. (A. N. H. Glover)

30) Unlike the stovepipe chimney as fitted to 30520 (caption 20 – page 14) this type of funnel really suited the design of the LSWR 'Greyhound' T9 Class 4-4-0's. No 30707 from 71B Bournemouth, awaits departure from Southampton (Central) with a semi-fast passenger to Bournemouth (West) via the 'old line' in April 1958. (A. C. Ingram)

31) A crowded scene at 71A Eastleigh on 22nd April 1956. Most roads are occupied by a variety of different classes, with the exception of two towards the left of the picture. Identified are SR *King Arthur* Class 4-6-0 No 30789 *Sir Guy*, sister (or brother) engine No 30796 *Sir Dodinas le Savage* and ex. works SR H15 Class 4-6-0 No 30474. (N. E. Preedy)

32) The photographer must have had a very steady hand and nerves of steel as SR *Schools* Class 4-4-0 No 30909 *St. Paul's*, from 73A Stewarts Lane, fitted with a multiple jet blastpipe and large diameter chimney, bears down on him near to Herne Bay with an express to London in August 1957. Pieces of various equipment lying around the track herald the forthcoming Kent Coast electrification. (Brian Coates)

33) Unlike the London sheds, 75A Brighton remained a place where pre-grouping steam was common, almost to the end. In May 1956, E4 Class 0-6-2T No 32468, waiting at the shed exit signal, has only ex. LBSCR engines for company. They are K Class 2-6-0 No 32338 and another E4 Class 0-6-2T (unidentified), but modern times intrude in the shape of a 1938 2HAL electric, arriving from Portsmouth. (Peter Hay)

34) With its paintwork glistening, SR *King Arthur* Class 4-6-0 No 30457 *Sir Bedivere* stands light engine at Southampton (Central) station at 1.25 pm on a March day in 1958. *Sir Bedivere*, was, at this moment of time, allocated to 70D Basingstoke. It survived in service until withdrawal from Nine Elms in May 1961, and was scrapped at Eastleigh Works two months later. (A. C. Ingram)

35) The remote Southern Region outpost of Sheerness-on-Sea is the venue for this LMS Class 2 2-6-2T No 41313 in begrimed external condition at the head of coaching stock on 21st March 1959. 41313, based at 73E Faversham was destined to end its days on the Southern in November 1965 after spells at Ashford, Barnstaple, Brighton and Eastleigh. (N. L. Browne)

36) Ex. SECR D1 Class 4-4-0 No 31489, a visitor from 74D Tonbridge, simmers in the shed yard at 75B Redhill on 25th May 1957. Note the rather primitive double wheel controlled water column adjacent to 31489. This locomotive was to remain at Tonbridge until transfer to 73B Bricklayers Arms in July 1960 where it remained in service until condemned in November 1961. (A. N. H. Glover)

37) Bright sunshine on an early summer's day helps to highlight the appearance of SR Maunsell Class U 4P3F 2-6-0 No 31808 as it hisses impatiently by the coal stage at 74C Dover on 3rd June 1951. Dover, re-coded 73H in September 1958 was to remain open to steam until December 1961. In 1959 it was one of a number of Southern sheds to receive a batch of WR Pannier tanks. (A. N. H. Glover)

38) Freight traffic on the Southern was very scarce, compared to other regions and as a consequence were rarely photographed. SR N Class 4P5F 2-6-0 No 31411 from 73A Stewarts Lane rattles a lengthy coal train from Snowdon Colliery, towards the camera near to Selling in March 1957. Selling is situated between Canterbury and Faversham. (Brian Coates)

39) Complete with insignia and flags, BR *Britannia* Class 4-6-2 No 70004 *William Shakespeare*, the pride of Stewarts Lane, is in faultless condition as it accelerates away from Folkestone after a signal check in March 1954 at the head of the down *Golden Arrow*. The frosty atmosphere is assisting the steam and smoke effect within this photograph. (Brian Coates)

40) It is a good thing that the Second World War did not last any longer than it did, otherwise all the steam locomotives in Britain might have ended up looking like this. Nevertheless the Q1 Class 0-6-0's 'Spam-Cans' were very powerful and purpose built for the urgent jobs in hand from 1942 onwards. No 33020 rests between duties at Eastleigh shed on 15th August 1951. (A. N. H. Glover)

41) Having already stated the rarity of photographs of freight trains on the Southern, another one is captured on film in July 1952. The evening sunlight glints off the boiler of SR N Class 2-6-0 No 31875 as it throws a pall of smoke into the sky whilst climbing past Bearsted, near Maidstone with a heavy van train bound for Dover. (Brian Coates)

42) An impressive signal gantry overlooks a line-up of passenger engine power at Ashford during July 1958. In the foreground SR *Schools* Class 4-4-0 No 30912 *Downside* (74B Ramsgate) waits for the road into the M.P.D. In the centre is an unidentified *WC/BB* Rebuilt 4-6-2 which has just arrived from London whilst in the background SR *Schools* Class 4-4-0 No 30924 *Haileybury* (73B Bricklayers Arms) backs into the station with a stopping train for Ramsgate. (Brian Coates)

CHAPTER THREE — EASTERN REGION

43) A small group of enthusiasts and railwaymen are mesmerised by the sight of LNER Thompson B1 Class 4-6-0 No 61079 as it slips to a standstill in Peterborough North Station in May 1958. The cylinder cocks are cleared and 61079 will soon be speeding on its way to Cleethorpes with an express from Kings Cross. 61079, its numberplate and shedcode both smartened up by the use of white paint was allocated to 40B Immingham where it remained until withdrawn from service in June 1962. (A. C. Ingram)

44) As a long train of mainly empty 'lowfit' wagons trundles past on an adjoining line, LNER J6 Class 0-6-0 No 64220 (35A New England) wheezes out of Spalding with a very short goods in April 1956. Between the trains we can see the rather unusual layout of Spalding station, with each direction served by a pair of platform lines. (Peter Hay)

45) A smartly turned out LNER J20 Class 0-6-0 No 64685 based at 30C Bishops Stortford departs serenely from Bury St. Edmunds with an R.C.T.S. Railtour of East Anglia on 6th September 1953. 64685 and Bishops Stortford shed demised almost at the same time with the former being withdrawn in October 1960 and the shed closing completely the following month. (N. E. Preedy)

46) Out of a total of 733 War Department Austerity Class 8F 2-8-0's only one was named, No 90732 *Vulcan*. For many spotters this locomotive was an 'elusive beast', rarely seen or photographed. In September 1959 90732 *Vulcan* was to be seen in the yard of its home shed at 36A Doncaster. Transferred to 36C Frodingham in February 1960 *Vulcan* was to be withdrawn in September 1962. (N. E. Preedy)

47) Newly transferred to 18A Toton from 9E Trafford Park, LMS Class 8F 2-8-0 No 48698 rattles a train of empties under the massive girder bridge carrying the East Coast Main Line in October 1958. 48698 is on a duty on the line from Norwich to Leicester and has not long departed from Peterborough East which at one time belonged to the Great Eastern Railway. (A. C. Ingram)

48) A keen wind beats smoke down over the station at Cambridge as LNER 'Claud Hamilton' Class D16/3 4-4-0 No 62616 leaves one of the bay platforms with a local passenger train. 62616 a local engine, is hauling carriages of LNER vintage on 5th July 1952 but on the left there is a glimpse of much older GER stock (Peter Hay)

49) A trio of ex. GER locomotives simmer in peace on a lovely Spring day on 24th May 1958 some distance from the straight shed at 30E Colchester. From left to right are J20 Class 0-6-0 No 64699 (31B March), J17 Class 0-6-0 No 65525 (32A Norwich) and J19 Class 0-6-0 No 64660 a local engine. Colchester shed closed to steam in December 1959. (F. Hornby)

50) Bearing a military style stance, a smartly dressed gentleman braves the freezing conditions to admire the departure of an immaculate LNER B1 Class 4-6-0 No 61288 as it leaves Lincoln Central with a passenger train on 27th February 1954. The compact church in the background helps with the character of this fine photograph. (G. Wood)

51) A panoramic view of the water tank, yard and four road straight shed at 31C Kings Lynn as seen from the station platform on 13th September 1958. All the engines which are visible are of Great Eastern origin. Only one can be identified – J17 Class 0-6-0 No 65526, a native of this depot. One can almost feel the urge to get into this picture, run across the tracks and disappear into the shed with a notebook. (F. Hornby)

52) Wath-on-Dearne was a sub-shed of Mexborough. One of the huge LNER Q1 Class 0-8-0 Tanks poses for the camera early in 1957. This particular locomotive No 69933 was allocated to 50C Selby, miles from home. One can only guess by its external condition that it had recently been out-shopped at Gorton and was in transit to its home shed on this particular day. (N. E. Preedy)

53) An almost deserted scene at the normally busy station of Hatfield on 20th September 1958. A Ministry of Supply WD Class 8F 'Bed-Iron' 2-8-0 No 90165 (34E New England) clanks out of a siding with an exchange freight. How this scene will have changed since 1958 with steam and the depot gone to be replaced by diesels, overhead wires and colour signals instead of semaphores. (F. Hornby)

54 Despite the immaculate external condition, the working life of LNER 'Sandringham' B17 Class 4-6-0 No 61645 *The Suffolk Regiment* is almost at an end. 61645, its tender packed to capacity is ready for the road in the yard of its home shed at 31B March in July 1958 seven months before withdrawal. Between January 1957 and June 1960 March had twenty of these engines at different times. (N. E. Preedy)

55) Peterborough in its prime had two steam sheds, at New England and Spital Bridge. This is a typical scene at the former during 1958. Most of the engines on view are either LNER V2 Class 2-6-2's or BR Class 9F 2-10-0's. The nearest 9F is identified as No 92144 based at New England. To the right of 92144 is LNER B1 Class 4-6-0 No 61094 a visitor from 41A Darnall (Sheffield). (A. C. Ingram)

56) Hertford (North) station (E.R.) on 20th September 1958. Hemmed in between a water column and a duet of small triple semaphores, each on single wooden posts is LNER N2 Class 0-6-2T No 69572 from 34B Hornsey. The train it is hauling, bunker-first, is the 1.31 pm local passenger to Kings Cross, the final destination being displayed on the coal bunker. (F. Hornby)

57) On summer Saturdays in the early 1950's every other train at Cambridge seemed to be in charge of an LNER D16/3 Class 4-4-0. Gresley carriages, some still in varnished teak, formed the majority of the trains giving the station an almost pre-war look. No 62589 from 31B March is arriving with an up express on 5th July 1952 and will swing alongside this platform at the scissors cross-over half-way along its two-train length. (Peter Hay)

58) The two white headcode discs highlight the grubby condition of LNER B17/4 Class 5P4F 4-6-0 No 61648 *Arsenal* as it draws out of sidings and approaches Colchester station with an up empty stock train. Impending electrification draws nearer with the installation of masts for the overhead wires as seen on 24th May 1958. (F. Hornby)

59) One of the lesser well known classes designed by Gresley were the LNER K2 Class 2-6-0's all of which were allocated to depots on the Eastern and Scottish Regions. One of its number, No 61762 from 40F Boston is in a line-up of dead locomotives in the yard at 40A Lincoln on 19th September 1954. Introduced in 1914, 61762 was taken out of service from Boston in June 1959. (F. Hornby)

60) The pioneer LNER Gresley V2 Class 2-6-2 No 60800 *Green Arrow* basks in early Spring sunshine in the shed yard at 36A Doncaster on 12th April 1959. *Green Arrow*, a visitor from 34A Kings Cross, was withdrawn from there in August 1962 and is now owned by the National Railway Museum at York. Only eight of these fine locomotives were ever named. (A. N. H. Glover)

61) With a wisp of steam coming from the safety valves, BR Class 9F 2-10-0 No 92036 (34E New England) disturbs the peaceful countryside near to Newark on the East Coast Main Line with a loose-coupled freight on 11th July 1958. 92036 moved on to pastures new in September 1962 to 36A Doncaster. Then in the space of just over two years to withdrawal in December 1964 it moved no less than four more times to other sheds. (A. Wakefield)

CHAPTER FOUR — THE SOUTH WEST

62) With the double-chimney exhaust reverberating off the cutting and houses, GWR *County* Class 4-6-0 No 1010 *County of Caernarvon* (83D Laira) has a good head of steam despite what appears to be a tender full of slack as it accelerates towards Mutley Tunnel after leaving Plymouth (North Road) with the up *Mayflower* to Paddington on 19th June 1959. The haulage of crack expresses on a regular basis in this part of England was soon to be a thing of the past with the onrushing fleet of *Warship* diesel-hydraulics to the area. (Terry Nicholls)

63) A visiting Pacific from 72A Exmouth Junction looks in fine external fettle after being serviced at 72B Salisbury on 6th September 1959. SR Rebuilt *Merchant Navy* Class 4-6-2 No 35011 *General Steam Navigation* parades its handsome and powerful lines in the shed yard. Rebuilt in July 1959, 35011 was withdrawn in February 1966 and after many years of storage at Barry now awaits preservation. (N. E. Preedy)

64) Three examples of the 'Big Four' amalgamate in this picture taken in the yard of the small depot at Andover, a sub-shed of 71A Eastleigh, on 14th May 1955. Nearest to the camera is LMS Class 4 2-6-4T No 42100 (75F Tunbridge Wells), with GWR 4300 Class 2-6-0 No 6341 (82C Swindon) alongside. Behind 6341 is SR U Class 2-6-0 No 31634 – home shed unknown. (F. Hornby)

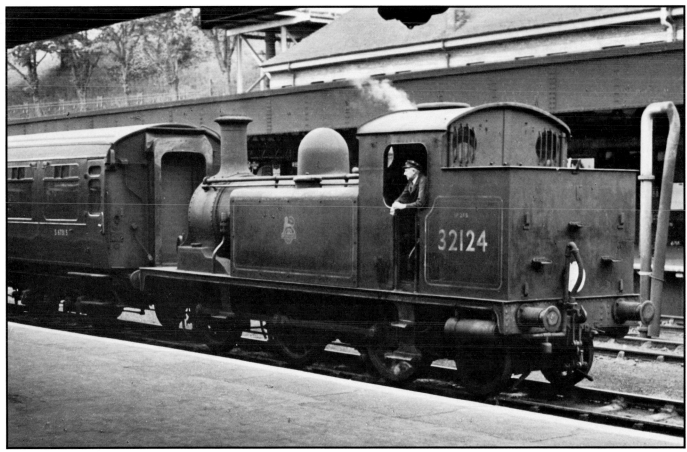

65) The driver of Stroudley SR Class E1/R 0-6-2T No 32124 takes it easy on the footplate of his charge on a through road at Exeter (Central) in August 1958. This and other members of the class were allocated to 72A Exmouth Junction and were employed in the main on shunting and banking duties. 32124 was taken out of service in January 1959. (H. H. Bleads).

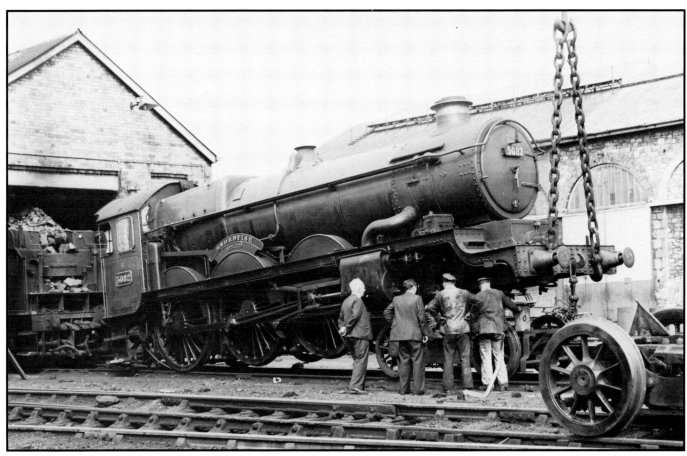

66) At first glance it looks as though GWR *Castle* Class 4-6-0 No 5082 *Swordfish* is trying to emulate its famous flying counterpart by attempting a short vertical take-off from 83A Newton Abbot in August 1956. At least one of the four railwaymen must have great faith in the strength of the twin chains which are holding this 81A Old Oak Common engine in the air whilst they attempt to diagnose the problem afflicting *Swordfish*. (G. W. Sharpe)

67) Dorchester shed on 22nd May 1957 not long before complete closure. On view are SR Unrebuilt *West Country* Class 4-6-2 No 34020 *Seaton* (70A Nine Elms), SR Unrebuilt *Battle of Britain* Class 4-6-2 No 34110 *66 Squadron* (71B Bournemouth) and an unidentified SR Q Class 0-6-0. Dorchester was coded 71C until 1955 thence becoming a sub-shed of 71B Bournemouth. (A. N. H. Glover)

68) A group of workers prepare to board an express which is arriving at Lostwithiel deep in former Great Western territory in Cornwall in June 1956. In charge of the express is GWR *Grange* Class 4-6-0 No 6821 *Leaton Grange*, from 83D Laira (Plymouth). Lostwithiel is situated on the Paddington-Penzance main line between Bodmin Road and St Austell. (G. W. Sharpe)

69) Tank engine power surrounds a lone Bulleid Pacific in the yard at 72A Exmouth Junction shed on 9th July 1956. At the forefront of this line-up is SR 02 Class 0-4-4T No 30232, a local engine destined for withdrawal in September 1959. Behind 30232 is SR Unrebuilt *West Country* Class 4-6-2 No 34004 *Yeovil*, another local engine, later rebuilt in February 1958. (F. Hornby)

70) The driver and fireman of SR Adams 0415 Class 4-4-2T No 30583 pose for the camera from the footplate of their engine prior to departing light engine from Lyme Regis on 2nd September 1952. 30583 and the two other members of this class, allocated to 72A Exmouth Junction made the branch to Lyme Regis their own for a great number of years. 30583 was withdrawn in July 1961 and is now preserved on the Bluebell Railway. (A. N. H. Glover)

71) The driver and porter are about to exchange single line tokens at Glastonbury on the former Somerset & Dorset Joint Railway on 12th September 1958. S. & D.J.R. built Class 3F 0-6-0 No 43216 (82G Templecombe) is hauling the 1.40 pm local passenger train to Highbridge. Glastonbury station and the branch to Highbridge closed in 1966. (N. L. Browne)

72) A steamy scene in the shed yard at 72B Salisbury on 2nd June 1951. Still carrying the logo of its former owners is SR 700 Class 0-6-0 No 691 (30691), a visitor from 72A Exmouth Junction and not as yet fitted with a front numberplate. To the right of 30691 is SR H15 Class 4-6-0 No 30330 a native of Salisbury shed. As can be seen in the background the shed building is constructed mainly from wood. (A. N. H. Glover)

73) The Western Region authorities must have been short of motive power on 23rd August 1959 as the rather unusual combination of GWR 4500 Class 2-6-2T No 5554 and GWR 5700 Class 0-6-0PT No 3736 prepare to leave Taunton with a through express bound for Minehead. Despite the fact that 5554 is carrying a Westbury shedplate it had just been transferred to Taunton. (Terry Nicholls)

74) Swindon Works, still at its zenith in June 1957. Nearest the camera and ex. works is GWR 4300 Class 2-6-0 No 7341, fully lined out in green livery, allocated to 84B Oxley and newly renumbered from 9319. Next to 7341 is sister engine No 6313 from 81C Southall. In the background is a former Taff Vale Railway 0-6-2T No 376. (W. Potter)

75) A trio of ex. Great Western locomotives as photographed in the shed yard at 82A Bristol (Bath Road) from one of the platforms at Temple Meads station in 1958. From left to right are *County* Class 4-6-0 No 1007 *County of Brecknock* (83F Truro), carrying the *Merchant Venturer* headboard, 5700 Class 0-6-0PT No 4603 and *Castle* Class 4-6-0 No 4073 *Caerphilly Castle* (86C Cardiff – Canton). (E. A. Elias)

76) An elderly SR M7 Class 0-4-4T No 30131 pushes an equally old set of vintage carriages out of Yeovil Town station and heads for Yeovil Junction in August 1959. This service was the preserve of a number of these engines for many years and they were based at the nearby shed, coded 72C. They were replaced during 1963 by ex. Great Western types. (H. H. Bleads)

77) The down *Torbay Express* has left the main West of England line at Aller Junction, Newton Abbot and is heading for its journey's end at Kingswear on 27th June 1958. A clean GWR *Castle* Class 4-6-0 No 5074 *Hampden* (81A Old Oak Common) nears Torre station beyond Aller with a rake of chocolate and cream coaches. *Hampden* is paired with a straight-sided tender. (J. Head)

78) A once timeless scene as captured on film on 13th September 1958. The elderly omnibus in the left of the picture and the small locomotive and train are reminiscent of the days of 'St. Trinians' and the 'Titfield Thunderbolt'. Ex. S. & D.J.R. Class 3F 0-6-0 No 43218 (82G Templecombe) stands on weed strewn tracks at Burnham-on-Sea as it awaits departure with a local passenger train. The station had closed in 1951. (N. L. Browne)

79) Piles of ash and coal litter the small depot yard at 72E Barnstaple on 18th May 1957. Steam hisses gently from the cylinder cocks of LMS Ivatt Class 2 2-6-2T No 41295 seen in company with another local engine in the shape of SR M7 Class 0-4-4T No 30256. Barnstaple became the property of the WR in 1963. Recoded 83F it closed completely in September 1964. (A. N. H. Glover)

80) An immaculate SR Unrebuilt *West Country* Class 4-6-2 No 34106 *Lydford* draws into Templecombe station with an up express in the summer of 1959. Transferred to 72A Exmouth Junction in January 1958 from 71B Bournemouth, *Lydford*, which remained in unrebuilt form all of its working life, was eventually withdrawn from there in September 1964. (A. C. Ingram)

81) 22A Bristol (Barrow Road) LMS *Jubilee* Class 4-6-0 No 45572 *Eire* takes liquid refreshment at the Birmingham end of Derby (Midland) station in July 1952 whilst in charge of a York-Bristol express. Despite the influx of diesels on this route in the early sixties many of these fine locomotives were still to be seen on these workings on a regular basis until the end of 1964. Transferred to 89A Shrewsbury in October 1961 *Eire* moved on briefly to 1A Willesden in January 1964 before condemnation the following month. It was cut up not far from where this picture was taken, by Loom's of Spondon. (L. Brownhill)

82) Further down the same line to the south-west of Birmingham, an LMS Unrebuilt *Patriot* Class 4-6-0 No 45509 *The Derbyshire Yeomanry* speeds into the shadows created by the late afternoon sunshine as it passes through Barnt Green with a down Bristol express on 26th June 1954. The station bookstall and upper quadrant signals are now long gone. (G. Wood)

83) On the fringes of the north-east Midlands was Staveley G.C. shed coded 38D which was altered to 41H in February 1958. On shed in the yard on 7th April 1957 is a Robinson GC Class 04/8 2-8-0 No 63801, rebuilt with an 01 boiler and firebox and a resident of this depot. Accompanying 63801 are two WD Class 8F 2-8-0's one of which is 90025 from 38A Colwick. (F. Hornby)

84) Ex. Midland Railway Class 3F & 4F 0-6-0's dominate part of the shed yard at 21A Saltley in March 1959, all of which are in a grubby condition. Two are identified as Nos 43484 and 43594, both local inhabitants of the shed. They were used mainly for local goods traffic and on banking duties up the Camp Hill avoiding line past St. Andrews football stadium. (H. H. Bleads)

85) GWR *Modified Hall* Class 4-6-0 No 6989 *Wightwick Hall*, sporting an 85A Worcester shedplate is attached to the stock of the 4.35 pm stopping train to Birmingham (Snow Hill) on a centre road at Worcester (Shrub Hill) on 2nd June 1957. Within a matter of days 6989 was to be transferred to 85C Hereford. *Wightwick Hall* is now preserved at Quainton Road. (H. H. Bleads).

86) The LNER penetrated Derbyshire with lines from Nottingham, seeking coal traffic and they were among the last places where the former GNR J6 Class 0-6-0's regularly worked passenger train services. A Nottingham to Derby train is entering Basford (North) on 5th September 1957 behind No 64200 (38A Colwick). Behind, there are connections to the former GCR London extension lines. (Peter Hay)

87) 38A Colwick was a massive freight orientated depot within close proximity to Nottingham. One of its legions of WD Class 8F 2-8-0's No 90161 is seen at rest near to a couple of oil storage tanks in the yard of the shed on 30th September 1956. Recoded 40E in February 1958, Colwick was transferred to the LMR in January 1966 becoming 16B. It closed to steam in December of the same year. (A. N. H. Glover)

88) Although the name of Birmingham (Snow Hill) has recently been reborn it is nothing like the proud place it once was. Taking a centre road through the old station, at 4.30 pm according to the clock, is 84B Oxley based 4300 Class 2-6-0 No 5312 on a down ballast train in July 1955. 5312 did not have much of a future being condemned in October 1958. (R. S. Carpenter)

89) With the still to be seen massive signalbox dominating the background an ex. works former LNW Class 7F 0-8-0 No 49428 from 9A Longsight (Manchester) is at the head of a rake of empty cattle trucks at Shrewsbury in May 1957. Like the LNW steam locomotives, cattle trucks are now a thing of the past with today's modern railway having no room for either of them. (G. W. Sharpe)

90) Like Birmingham (Snow Hill), the other major station in the second city is still with us, much changed of course and to the worse, being a concrete monolith with railway tracks. Waiting to depart from New Street on 1st May 1957 with a Wolverhampton (High Level) to London (Euston) express is LMS *Jubilee* Class 4-6-0 No 45740 *Munster* (1A Willesden) paired with a small tender. (G. H. Wilson)

91) An 89C Machynlleth GWR 2251 Class 0-6-0 No 2219 finds itself in the shed yard at 85B Gloucester (Horton Road) on 6th October 1951. Looking ex. works, with the British Railways logo on the tender 2219 may well have been on its way home from Swindon. In the background is one of the rapidly diminishing *Star* Class 4-6-0's. (D. K. Jones)

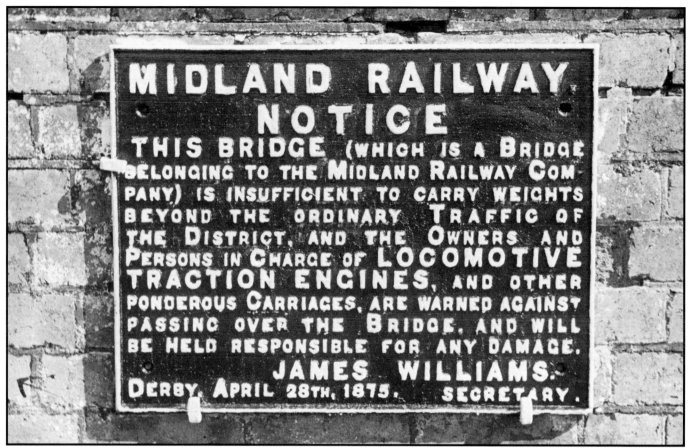

92) Like many other massive institutions the railways had a plethora of signs and notices forbidding the general public to do this, that and the other. It is a wonder that they did not go so far as to state 'do not stroke the station cat' or 'do not throw stones at this notice'. This photograph taken at Hinton-on-the-Green between Ashchurch and Evesham in April 1959 speaks for itself. (H. H. Bleads)

93) An unusual photograph as taken by the fireman of GWR 2800 Class 2-8-0 No 2867 at Toddington between Stratford-upon-Avon and Cheltenham whilst waiting for the road in a siding with a freight in June 1956. Toddington station closed in 1960 and is now the site of several preservation schemes including the restoration of a number of steam locomotives. (L. C. Jacks)

94) The ex. LNWR goods yard dominates this panoramic scene taken at Walsall in the heart of the West Midlands – circa 1957, looking towards the Bescot direction. In the foreground is a mass of signal rods and trackwork with an impressive gantry of semaphores in the distance. In the centre background two steam locos are coupled together and to the right of the picture is an LNW 0-8-0. (R. S. Carpenter)

95) Two generations of ex. MR freight power wait for the road at Chesterfield on 6th September 1957. Nearest to the camera is a rebuilt Johnson Class 3F 0-6-0 No 43321 (55E Normanton). Behind 43321 is Class 4F 0-6-0 No 43987 from 55B Stourton. The contraption on the handrail by the smokebox of each locomotive is the vacuum brake. (Peter Hay)

96) A very presentable GWR *Hall* Class 4-6-0 No 5921 *Bingley Hall* based at the local shed awaits departure from the modernised station at Banbury with a local passenger bound for Birmingham (Snow Hill) in June 1959. *Bingley Hall* was allocated to Banbury from January 1958 until June 1960 when it was re-allocated to 84E Tyseley before moving south to 82D Westbury three months later. (H. H. Bleads)

97) LMS Class 5 4-6-0 No 44683 carrying a local passenger headlamp has its work cut out at Derby on 6th June 1956 in charge of what is presumably a departmental coach. 44683 a 5A Crewe (North) engine for many years, moved to 5B Crewe (South) in June 1965. After further transfers to Springs Branch Wigan and Lostock Hall in 1967 it was withdrawn in April 1968. (N. L. Browne)

98) A modest amount of sulphur drifts from the chimney of BR Class 4 4-6-0 No 75035 at rest in the yard of Cheltenham shed on 30th August 1953. This four road depot with a quite spacious yard had been a sub-shed of Gloucester (Horton Road) since about 1936. Opened in 1907 it closed completely in October 1963. (N. L. Browne)

99) Strings of locomotives coupled together often came into Crewe station from the North shed to await their trains as shown here by LMS *Coronation* Class 4-6-2 No 46246 *City of Manchester* which is piloting LMS Class 5 4-6-0 No 45276 on 31st December 1955. *City of Manchester* still has a sloping smokebox, a left-over from its streamlined days. (J. D. Gomersall)

100) Bathed in bright summer sunshine, 9A Longsight (Manchester) LMS Class 5 4-6-0 No 45302 is ready for the road next to the shed building at 84G Shrewsbury in July 1958. 45302 had been transferred to Longsight from Crewe (North) the previous month. Before withdrawal in July 1967 it was to be re-allocated no less than six more times. (G. W. Sharpe)

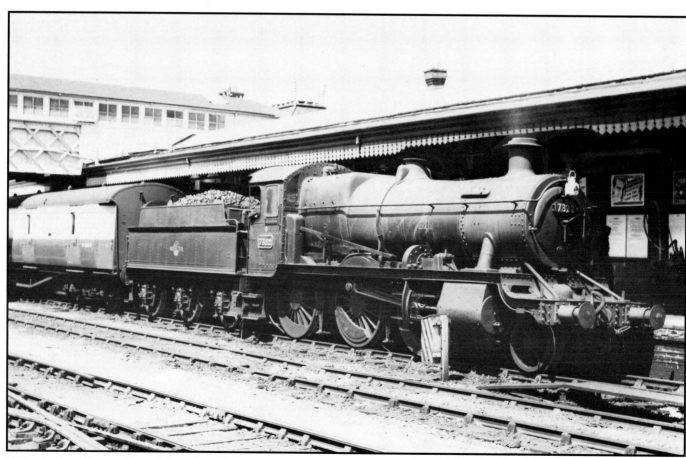

101) An 86E Severn Tunnel Junction GWR 4300 Class 2-6-0 No 7322 stands in Gloucester (Central) station at the head of a local passenger train on 19th July 1959. Renumbered from 9300 in April 1957, 7322 was to remain at Severn Tunnel shed until June 1961 when it went to 88J Aberdare. Three months later it arrived at its final shed 85B Gloucester (Horton Road) only to be withdrawn in November of the same year. (N. E. Preedy)

102) The route ahead is not totally clear as signified by the single raised upper quadrant in the background. LMS Stanier Crab Class 6P5F 2-6-0 No 42953, from 5B Crewe (South) passes the 'Smith Thompson-Houston' factory and cautiously approaches Rugby (Midland) station with a very long fitted freight from the north in November 1957. (A. C. Ingram)

103) Fresh from shops and re-coaled, LMS *Jubilee* Class 4-6-0 No 45630 *Swaziland* is waiting to be despatched to its home shed of 12A Carlisle (Upperby) from Crewe Works on 27th September 1953. During the late fifties *Swaziland* was based at 5A Crewe (North) and apart from a very brief spell at 8A Edge Hill (Liverpool) during 1958 it remained at Crewe being one of the first members of the class to be withdrawn, in November 1961. (G. Wood)

CHAPTER SIX — WALES

104) A reminder of how important the railways once were in rural areas and to small market towns. Out of sight in the left of this picture is the station at Oswestry with its links to far off important towns and cities. In the centre are two goods sheds, a number of wagons which helped to supply the community with all types of commodities, and a GWR 0-6-0 Pannier Tank shunts wagons in September 1959. Then came the Beeching Plan and railways in such places had to go regardless of the sometimes devastating effects. Oswestry was to lose everything, the station, goods yard, locomotive depot and workshop. (H. H. Bleads)

105) A solitary passenger (a railwayman) leans out of a window of a two coach push and pull train as it prepares to depart from Panteg and Griffithstown station with the 7.30 am Blaenavon to Newport working on 27th May 1956. Providing the rear end power is 86A Newport (Ebbw Junction) GWR 6400 Class 0-6-0PT No 6409. Panteg and Griffithstown station closed in 1962. (F. Hornby)

106) The end is almost nigh for a trio of ex. Cambrian Railways 'Dukedog' Class 4-4-0's as they lie in store with sacked chimney's on a back road at 89A Oswestry shed on 26th May 1957. They are, from left to right Nos 9010, 9026 and 9020 withdrawn in July, August and July 1957 respectively. All were scrapped at Swindon Works in August 1957. (F. Hornby)

107) A begrimed GWR 9400 Class 0-6-0PT No 9458 throws a pall of black smoke and steam into the Monmouthshire sky as it leaves New Tredegar with the 2.38 pm local to Machen on 6th June 1953. This line, originally owned by the Brecon and Merthyr Tydfil Junction Railway and its associated stations closed in 1962, yet another Beeching type victim. (F. Hornby)

108) Rebuilding work is in progress at one of the top passenger sheds in South Wales on 22nd May 1955, 86C Cardiff (Canton). Carrying a *not to be moved* board on the bufferbeam is one of the immaculately kept fleet of Canton GWR *Castle* Class 4-6-0's No 5054 *Earl of Ducie*. Built in June 1936 *Earl of Ducie* was to be withdrawn in October 1964 after over twenty-eight years of service. (F. Hornby)

109) GWR Churchward 4200 Class 2-8-0T No 5216 by the coal stage at 87B Duffryn Yard on 9th July 1950. In the early 1900's the developing coal traffic in South Wales with its short haul trips from pithead to port or power stations brought about the need for a powerful tank engine. A total of 205 of these engines were built and 54 were later rebuilt as 2-8-2 Tanks. (A. N. H. Glover)

110) LMS Class 2 2-6-0 No 46520 from 89B Brecon coasts into Machen station, overlooked by mountainous terrain deep in South Wales, on a Newport to Brecon local passenger train on 21st May 1955. Less than a handful of passengers wait to board this train. 46520 moved on to pastures new when Brecon became a sub-shed in November 1959. (N. L. Browne)

111) Three ex. Cambrian Railways 'Dukedog' Class 4-4-0's are stabled on the coaling road at Aberystwyth shed on 17th July 1955. The centre 'Dukedog' is No 9017 which was to survive in service at 89C Machynlleth until October 1960 and is now preserved on the Bluebell Railway. Aberystwyth, a sub-shed of Machynlleth closed in April 1965. (W. Potter)

112) The 4.35 pm Lydney to Sharpness Auto-Train runs into Severn Bridge station being propelled by an unidentified GWR 1400 Class 0-4-2T, probably based at 85B Gloucester (Horton Road) in June 1959. This station, once the property of the Severn and Wye Joint Railway was closed in 1960 after a ship had damaged the bridge to Sharpness beyond financial repair. (H. H. Bleads)

113) GWR 5700 Class 0-6-0PT No 9664 (86A Newport – Ebbw Junction) takes a breather between station pilot duties at Newport (High Street) on 27th May 1956. Built at Swindon in 1948 by British Railways 9664 was to survive in revenue earning service until May 1964. A member of the crew also takes it easy on the footplate with his feet up and reading a newspaper. (F. Hornby)

114) Former Taff Vale Railway 0-6-2T No 373, rebuilt with a Great Western tapered boiler, is prepared at 88B Cardiff East Dock on 25th August 1957 for its final journey to Swindon and an appointment with the cutting torch. Cardiff East Dock had a number of pre-grouping locomotives on its books, the last being withdrawn in October 1957. (W. Potter)

115) The driver and fireman of GWR 2251 Class 0-6-0 No 2200 lean out of the cab of their charge as it enters Dovey Junction station on the old Cambrian section of the Western Region on 17th July 1958. 2200 an 89C Machynlleth engine is hauling the 6.45 pm to Aberystwyth. Built in June 1938 and withdrawn in September 1962 it was not cut up until June 1964. (F. Hornby)

116) An extremely grubby ex. Cambrian Railways 'Dukedog' Class 4-4-0 No 9014 waits for its next rostered working in the yard of its home shed at 84J Croes Newydd, Wrexham on 30th August 1959. The tender of 9014 is stacked to the brim with huge lumps of coal. Built at Swindon in August 1937 this engine along with 9017 were the last two members of the class in service, being withdrawn in October 1960. (F. Hornby)

117) Ex. LNWR 1P Class 2-4-2T No 46604 was a relic at 7B Bangor shed of the days when it provided power for passenger trains over several branches running up into the valleys of Snowdonia behind the North Wales coast. In August 1952 it was working out its last days as shed pilot. It was numbered in a bold block letter style which appeared briefly at the end of the 1940's. (Peter Hay)

118) The former Taff Vale terminus at Cardiff (Bute Road) is the setting for this picture of GWR 4500 Class 2-6-2T No 5534 with a Cardiff (Queen Street) auto-train on 21st May 1955. 5534 was based at Cardiff (Radyr) until July 1958 when it moved on to 86G Pontypool Road. In January 1960 it was sent to 83E St. Blazey where it ended its days in September of the same year. (F. Hornby)

119) Heavy freight engine power in the depot yard at 86A Newport (Ebbw Junction) in the shape of GWR 2800 Class 2-8-0 No 2809 from far off Devon, being allocated to 83A Newton Abbot. Behind 2809 is an unidentified WD Class 8F 2-8-0 on 22nd May 1955. Between January 1957 and withdrawal in January 1960, 2809 served at no less than four different depots. (F. Hornby)

120) Complete with headboard and freshly painted express lamps GWR *Manor* Class 4-6-0 No 7802 *Bradley Manor* (89C Machynlleth) pilots an unidentified member of the GWR 4300 Class 2-6-0's at Machynlleth on the *Cambrian Coast Express* in May 1959. The external condition of *Bradley Manor* is in stark contrast to that of the 2-6-0. Withdrawn in November 1965 *Bradley Manor* is currently being restored on the Severn Valley Railway. (N. E. Preedy)

121) With its exhaust roaring GWR *Castle* Class 4-6-0 No 5049 *Earl of Plymouth* struggles up the stiff gradient into Llanvihangel station with a heavy north-west express in April 1954. Llanvihangel situated between Abergavenny and Pontrilas closed in 1958. Waiting in the loop for a path between trains is WD Class 8F 2-8-0 No 90179 on a loose fitted goods. (G. W. Sharpe)

122) A Hawksworth 1600 Class 0-6-0PT No 1643 (built Swindon 1951) from Danygraig, Swansea is seen in the shed yard at Duffryn Yard, Port Talbot on 10th May 1953. The first of these locos did not appear until 1949 and they were to be the last locos of Great Western design to be constructed at Swindon. Behind 1643 is GWR 5700 Class 0-6-0PT No 6719. (A. N. H. Glover)

123) A plume of steam rises into the air from the safety valves of BR Class 5 4-6-0 No 73016 as it backs the empty stock of a local passenger train into Sheffield (Midland) station on 12th May 1956. The overall roof between platforms five and six was being removed to be replaced later by a modern platform canopy structure. 73016 was allocated to 19B Millhouses which was recoded 41C in February 1958. When Millhouses closed on 31st December 1961 73016 was transferred to another Sheffield area shed, this time to 41D Canklow. (J. D. Gomersall)

124) The prosperity of the old NER is reflected in this view of the spacious layout at Hull with the fine Paragon station behind. We can also see it in the high, wide and handsome profile of the compartment third which is next to C12 Class 4-4-2T No 67397, leaving on a local service on 29th August 1952. In the background is a G5 Class 0-4-4T. (Peter Hay)

125) The huge cast iron water tower with its ornate design dominates the skyline at 54B Tyne Dock shed on 15th June 1952. One of the massive purpose built NER Raven designed Q7 Class 0-8-0's, first introduced in 1919, No 63463 lies idle in the yard of its home shed. They were employed mostly on the hefty iron ore trains which used to ply back and forth between Tyne Dock and Consett. (A. N. H. Glover)

126) An unknown East Coast Main Line express makes a fine start southwards from York on 30th August 1952. The engine is LNER A3 Class 4-6-2 No 60040 *Cameronian* and the LNER coaches are mostly of Gresley design, some still in varnished teak and others in the new red and white livery for corridor stock. The goods lines avoiding York station go off to the left beyond the bridge. (Peter Hay)

127) Steam hisses gently from the safety valves of NER G5 Class 0-4-4T No 67315 as it waits with a brakevan at Malton on the North Yorkshire Moors on 11th June 1956. This locomotive was built in December 1900 and withdrawn exactly fifty-eight years later. Malton, at one time possessed its own shed, coded 50F which closed in April 1963. (F. Hornby)

128) The handsome profile of a Raven designed NER B16/1 Class 4-6-0 is clearly to be observed in this picture of No 61469 at rest in the yard of its home shed at 50C Selby on 29th June 1958. Upon closure of the shed in October 1959 61469 was transferred to 50A York where it ended its days in November 1960 being cut up at Darlington Works the same month. (A. N. H. Glover)

129) Amid the snows of winter on the Plain of York, a War Department 'Austerity' Class 8F 2-8-0 approaches Wetherby with a loose-coupled freight train from Gascoigne Wood Yard near Selby. The engine is No 90465 from 51B Newport and the date is 9th December 1955. (Peter Hay)

130) The chimney of LNER J26 Class 0-6-0 No 65760 (51B Newport) is seeking to make up for the lack of industrial smog at Thornaby on a sunny 11th August 1956. This class and the similar J27 Class 0-6-0's dominated freight working on Teesside for many years, moving legions of the distinctive ex. NER coal wagons like the one immediately in front of the engine. (Peter Hay)

131) LNER Thompson A1 Class 4-6-2 No 60130 *Kestrel* blackens the sky around Leeds (Holbeck) as it struggles with its heavy load of Pullman coaches and heads southwards with the up *Queen of Scots* bound for Kings Cross from Glasgow (Queen Street) on 21st July 1956. *Kestrel*, for many years a 56C Copley Hill locomotive survived until October 1965 being withdrawn from 56B Ardsley. (B. K. B. Green)

132) With safety valves lifting NER G5 Class 0-4-4T No 67297 simmers outside the straight running shed of its home depot at 54A Sunderland on 15th June 1952. Next to 67297 is one of Sunderland's massive NER A8 Class 4-6-2 Tanks No 69857. Behind both of these engines is the large roundhouse which was adjacent to the straight shed, but separate. (A. N. H. Glover)

133) There were only twenty members of the LNER N10 Class 0-6-2 Tanks and as they were to be found at work only in the north-east they were unfamiliar to most railway photographers. On 13th August 1956 No 69093 was piloting at Stella Gill in County Durham, a duty which included using the 1 in 24 of Waldridge Bank rope-worked incline. 69093 was withdrawn in 1957 but the incline survived until 1969. (Peter Hay)

134) A local goods train rattles under the enclosed footbridge and passes through Selby on the East Coast Main Line behind NER J27 Class 0-6-0 No 65857 from the nearby local shed, on 28th August 1952. By this date many engines had still not received the first BR totem and had tenders lettered with BRITISH RAILWAYS. A small boy on the platform logs the number of 65857. (Peter Hay)

135) Complete with express code headlamps an LNER Gresley D49/2 'Shire' Class 4-4-0 No 62749 *The Cottesmore* is ready to take a return working to Leeds on an overcast 10th June 1956. The location is the shed yard at 50E Scarborough and *The Cottesmore* is a visitor from 50B Leeds (Neville Hill). Built in August 1933 it was withdrawn from Neville Hill in July 1958. (F. Hornby)

136) LNER A2/2 Class 4-6-2 No 60503 *Lord President* is photographed on an unknown working at Blaydon on the outskirts of Newcastle in August 1952. *Lord President* was one of a batch of six engines rebuilt by Thompson from the earlier Gresley P2 Class 2-8-2's and is equipped with an ugly rimless chimney and small smoke deflectors. (G. W. Sharpe)

137) A congested scene in the shed yard at 51E Stockton on 12th August 1956, with LNER B16 Class 4-6-0 No 61432 from 50B Leeds (Neville Hill) and LNER A5 Class 4-6-2T No 69838 among the pre-grouping engines resting that Sunday. This depot with a fairly large straight running shed closed completely on 14th June 1959. (Peter Hay)

138) The final and most powerful development of the ex. NER 0-8-0 coal engine design was the three cylinder Q7 Class. No 63465 is seen here banking an iron ore train from Tyne Dock to the steelworks at Consett on 13th August 1956, at Pelton. The line is now long defunct and when the steelworks closed at Consett, the town almost died. (Peter Hay)

139) With a rather bleak landscape as a backdrop, a partially fitted freight rattles through Beighton on the outskirts of Sheffield with an LMS Hughes 'Crab' Class 6P5F 2-6-0 No 42931 in charge on 22nd May 1959. This engine is well off the beaten track being allocated to 1A Willesden. The line through Beighton was once the property of the Manchester, Sheffield and Lincolnshire/GC Railways. (N. E. Preedy)

140) A compact and handsome looking NER J72 Class 0-6-0T No 68707 is seen at rest alongside the straight shed at 51A Darlington on 22nd June 1952. Transferred to 51C West Hartlepool in the mid-fifties it was to remain in service there until withdrawn in April 1962. To the right of 68707 is an ex. works WD Class 8F 2-8-0 resplendent in fresh black livery. (A. N. H. Glover)

141) Bingley station of Midland Railway origin is situated between Shipley and Keighley on the borders of the North-East and North-West. The sparsley populated station plays host to a two coach local working in the mid-fifties, powered by a 20F Skipton LMS Class 4 2-6-0 No 43112. (G. W. Sharpe)

CHAPTER EIGHT — THE NORTH WEST

142) The famous landmark of the tower at Blackpool dominates the background on 17th March 1957. In the foreground are Barton Wright ex. L & Y 0-4-4T No 480 built in July 1886 and withdrawn for carriage heating duties in November 1910 and Barton Wright ex. L & Y 0-4-4T No 910 built in 1885 and withdrawn in February 1910 for similar duties. Note the brackets on the side of the smokeboxes to support the long chimneys when going for overhaul. Both engines were scrapped on closure of Blackpool Central station in November 1964. (J. D. Gomersall)

143) Looking every inch a pedigree and proudly displaying a somewhat crookedly placed headboard LMS *Coronation* Class 4-6-2 No 46222 *Queen Mary* impatiently waits to leave Carlisle (Citadel) station with the up *Royal Scot* from Glasgow (Central) to London (Euston) in April 1957. *Queen Mary* was allocated to 66A Polmadie (Glasgow) until withdrawal in October 1963. (G. W. Sharpe)

144) Bright sunshine reflects off the fittings in the cab of ex. GC J11 Class 0-6-0 No 64297 which is in steam in the yard of its home shed at 9G Gorton in the heart of Manchester in 1958. Transferred from 40E Langwith Junction in January of this same year, this Robinson engine was condemned at Gorton in June 1959 and cut up at the nearby works three months later. (G. W. Sharpe)

145) The very pleasant heavily wooded location of Grange-over-Sands is the setting for this photograph of a Stanier LMS Class 8F No 48714 on shunting duties in August 1959. 48714 had not long been transferred to 8C Speke Junction from 8B Warrington. Grange-over-Sands is situated between Carnforth and Barrow on the former Furness Railway. (A. C. Ingram)

146) The maid of all work on the London Midland Region was the LMS Stanier Class 5 4-6-0. The class reached a total of 842 machines and all were withdrawn between November 1961 and August 1968. One of their number, a begrimed 45236 from 11A Barrow heads a semi-fast passenger near Hellifield on 20th June 1959. (G. W. Sharpe)

147) The immediate area around the concrete coaling plant at 26C Bolton is a hive of activity on 21st June 1958. Nearest to the camera is an LMS Fowler Class 7F 0-8-0 heavy freight engine No 49578. Although the shedplate is missing, 49578 is a visitor from 26B Agecroft and behind this engine is an ex. L & Y Class 3F 0-6-0, identity unknown. (N. L. Browne)

148) A member of the footplate crew of LMS Class 5 4-6-0 No 44845, allocated to 26A Newton Heath, enjoys a breather and the summer sunshine as his mount heads a motley collection of carriages which have been pressed into service on this Blackpool to Manchester (Victoria) relief express at Salwick station on 1st August 1959. (B. W. L. Brooksbank)

149) With a clear road ahead LMS Unrebuilt *Patriot* Class 4-6-0 No 45501 *St. Dunstan's* leaves a trail of murky exhaust as it storms through Handforth, passing the sidings in the process and heads for Crewe on 1st March 1953 with a Manchester (London Road) express bound for the West of England. *St. Dunstan's* was the property of 9A Longsight on this date. (R. W. Hinton)

150) Bright sunshine heralds the passing of LMS *Princess* Class 4-6-2 No 46201 *Princess Elizabeth* as it accelerates a heavy Glasgow (Central) to Birmingham (New Street) express through Moore on the West Coast Main Line between Warrington and Acton Bridge on 29th March 1959. *Princess Elizabeth* will be replaced by another locomotive at Crewe for the final leg to Birmingham. (R. W. Hinton)

151) An extremely grimy BR Class 2 2-6-0 No 78023 (depot unknown) passes a double LNW lower quadrant post with a four coach local passenger working at Heaton Mersey, near to Stockport on 17th June 1954. Between January 1957 and withdrawal in May 1967, 78023 served at Millhouses, Doncaster, Stratford, March, Barrow, Aintree, Nottingham, Gorton, Trafford Park and Bolton. (R. W. Hinton)

152) A gaggle of spotters of all ages observe the departure of LMS Class 5 4-6-0 No 45074, from 5B Crewe (South) as it leaves Manchester (Exchange) with empty stock on 28th February 1953. Many of the glass panels in the overall roof are missing and one can only hope they did not fall on to any unsuspecting passengers waiting below. (R. W. Hinton)

153) Framed by sunlight and shadow, one of the experimental LMS Class 5 4-6-0's No 44748 based at 9A Longsight (Manchester) prepares to depart from Stockport (Edgeley) on 1st June 1957 with an unknown express. 44748 was introduced in 1948 being fitted with Caprotti valve gear and Timken roller bearings. To the right of 44748 is LMS Class 4 2-6-4T No 42379 (9B Stockport). (R. W. Hinton)

154) Heavy repair work was often undertaken at comparatively small sheds which were often equipped with lifting gear for this very purpose. Separated from its tender and partially lifted into the air to receive attention at 9G Northwich on 25th March 1956 is ex. GCR Large 'Director' Class D11 4-4-0 No 62665 *Mons*. This locomotive was named after one of the famous battlefields of the First World War. (J. D. Gomersall)

155) In ex. works condition BR Class 3 2-6-2T No 82036 stands amidst a haze of steam and smoke in the yard of its new home at 6E Chester (West) on 20th August 1958. 82036 had been newly transferred to this shed from 82A Bristol (Bath Road). Upon closure of this depot in April 1960, 82036 was moved to the ex. LNWR shed at Chester, coded 6A. (M. S. Stokes)

156) Fresh from overhaul at Crewe works LMS *Princess* Class 4-6-2 No 46200 *The Princess Royal*, its home shed being 8A Edge Hill (Liverpool), is relegated to a menial duty by way of a running in turn on 23rd June 1956. *The Princess Royal* approaches the camera at Cheadle Hulme with a stopping train bound for Crewe. (R. W. Hinton)

157) Rival engine crews on former rival companies' locomotives spar side by side, split by the tidy flower arranged platform at Salwick on 1st August 1959. Both engines are hauling unidentified down relief expresses. In the left of the picture is LMS Class 5 4-6-0 No 44971 (6B Mold Junction) and on the right is LNER B1 Class 4-6-0 No 61281 (40E Colwick). (B. W. L. Brooksbank)

158) Looking well overdue for a visit to workshops BR *Britannia* Class 4-6-2 No 70033 *Charles Dickens* is in quite disgraceful external condition standing in the shed yard at 9E Trafford Park in 1958. *Charles Dickens* was allocated to 9A Longsight (Manchester) at this time but it was to become a resident of Trafford Park in February 1960. (N. E. Preedy)

159) Pleasant suburbia in high summer is provided for by the setting at Cheadle Hulme between Sandbach and Stockport in July 1958. LMS Class 5 4-6-0 No 45146 (9A Longsight – Manchester) glides into the station from the Crewe direction with a nine coach express bound for Manchester. The platforms at Cheadle Hulme are partially slabbed and partly constructed from wood. (J. D. Owens)

160) A tall, thin dome and a whistle perched on the cab roof give this ex. Lancashire & Yorkshire Railway Class 3F 0-6-0 No 52237 a distinctive skyline as it drifts through Bradley Fold station, light engine, on 13th August 1953. 52237 had lost its shedplate but probably lived at nearby 26C Bolton shed. Bradley Fold station between Bolton and Bury closed in 1970. (Peter Hay)

161) The ex. Great North of Scotland branch line from Fraserburgh to St. Combs had only three intermediate stations – Kirkton Bridge Halt, Philorth Bridge Halt and Cairnbulg. Standing at the latter on 11th August 1954 is a local passenger in the hands of the modern LMS Class 2 2-6-0 No 46460. This engine had helped to replace the older motive power but the famous cow-catcher was still in use. The branch line closed forever in 1965. (Peter Hay)

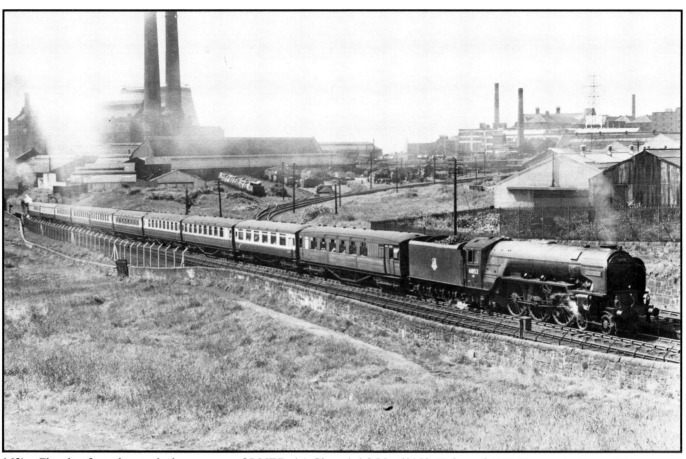

162) Clouds of smoke mark the passage of LNER A1 Class 4-6-2 No 60152 *Holyrood* (64B Haymarket) as, with rear end assistance, it climbs the 1 in 42 gradient from Glasgow (Queen Street) with an express for Edinburgh on 1st August 1953. The train is entirely composed of Gresley coaches, the first one still in varnished teak and the rest in red and cream. The second vehicle, with inset doors, is most unusual. (Peter Hay)

163) Piles of ash and shovels litter the yard at 65J Fort William on 26th June 1959. One of its resident 'old timers' ex. NBR J36 Class 0-6-0 No 65300 simmers in between duties. Most of Fort William's allocation of steam locomotives came from two classes – the LMS Class 5 4-6-0's and the LNER K1 Class 2-6-0's. 65300 survived at the shed until withdrawn in July 1962. (A. N. H. Glover)

164) Part of the depot building at 61A Kittybrewster in Aberdeen had been demolished by the time this photograph was taken on 26th June 1956. Present on this rain-soaked day is a smartly turned out and lined ex. NBR 'Glen' Class D34 4-4-0 No 62480 *Glen Fruin*, a resident of Kittybrewster with its name embellished on the wheel-splasher. (A. N. H. Glover)

165) The 'Old Order' at Edinburgh (Waverley) on 17th June 1958. The driver of LNER Gresley 'Shire' D49 Class 4-4-0 No 62715 *Roxburghshire* poses for the camera from the footplate. *Roxburghshire* and a small number of sister engines were allocated to 64A St. Margarets where the last example left in May 1961. This particular locomotive was withdrawn from 64A in June 1959. (F. Hornby)

166) Three members of the ex. Great North of Scotland Railway D40 Class 4-4-0's are present in this 6th August 1953 view of the east end of Elgin station. No 62264 is departing with the Craigellachie portion of the 5.50 pm to Aberdeen. In the distance another D40 is acting as station pilot, whilst on the right No 62272 is shunting the goods yard. (Peter Hay)

167) Ex. Caledonian Railway Class 3F 0-6-0 No 57552 from 66D Greenock is a stranger in the camp at 65B St. Rollox in May 1958. Judging by its external appearance it may well have not long been out of shops. Behind 57552 is an unidentified LMS *Jubilee* Class 4-6-0. St. Rollox shed, also known as Balornock, was about a twenty minute walk from the nearest station. (N. E. Preedy)

168) With heavy cloud overhead for company an LMS Class 4 2-6-4T No 42697 from 67D Ardrossan hurries a four coach local passenger train past Corkerhill in the suburbs of Glasgow on 27th August 1957. Corkerhill on the former Glasgow and South Western Railway between Glasgow (St. Enoch) and Paisley had its own motive power depot. (N. L. Browne)

169) Smoke curls lazily into the sea air at Dundee on 26th August 1957, from the chimney of former NBR Reid D30 Class 4-4-0 No 62438 *Peter Poundtext* from 62A Thornton Junction as steam hisses gently from the safety valves of the same locomotive, outside Dundee East shed. Time was running out for *Peter Poundtext* with condemnation only three months away. (N. L. Browne)

170) 65A Eastfield (Glasgow) based LNER K2 Class 2-6-0 No 61788 *Loch Rannoch* has the luxury of a side-window cab as it resides outside the primitive stone built sub-shed at Mallaig on 26th June 1959. They say that the camera never lies but from this angle *Loch Rannoch* looks far too big to fit inside the one road building. (A. N. H. Glover)

171) The cramped location of the Banff terminus would seem to have provided no room for a turntable. The branch engine on 4th August 1953, ex. CR Class 2F 0-4-4T No 55185 is backing towards the one road stone engine shed. In the extreme right of the picture, the all-over roof of the station can just be seen, a snug spot to wait for a train on a stormy day beside the rock-bound sea coast. The branch to Banff closed in 1964. (Peter Hay)

172 The cab of Pickersgill ex. Caledonian Railway Class 3P 4-4-0 No 54463 (60A Inverness) offers scant protection in the spartan conditions caused by a downpour on 19th June 1958. 54463 is awaiting departure on a northbound passenger working at ten o'clock in the evening. This locomotive remained at Inverness shed until sent to 63A Perth in April 1962. (N. L. Browne)

173) Possessing one of the longest names as applied to the LMS *Jubilee* Class 4-6-0's was No 45665 *Lord Rutherford of Nelson* seen here being prepared for the road in the yard of its home shed at 67A Corkerhill (Glasgow) in 1958. Eleven *Jubilee's* were based here during 1962 and most were put into store by the August at Corkerhill and Lugton prior to a mass withdrawal at the end of the year. (N. E. Preedy)

174)　Compact and strong would be a good description of LNER J83 Class 0-6-0T No 68447. Among its ancestors must surely have been Stroudley's Class E tank for the London, Brighton and South Coast Railway. Sharing the shed yard at 65A Eastfield (Glasgow) on 8th August 1953 are LNER B1 Class 4-6-0 No 61117 and LNER J72 Class 0-6-0T No 68733. (Peter Hay)

175)　The North British Railway pattern lattice-work footbridge throws strange shadows on to ex. NBR D30 Class 4-4-0 No 62436 *Lord Glenvarloch* (62C Dunfermline) as it pauses at Cowdenbeath (New) station with a lightweight 1.52 pm Thornton Junction to Dunfermline local passenger on 22nd April 1957. *Lord Glenvarloch* was withdrawn from Dunfermline in June 1959. (Peter Hay)

176) Two of the modern LNER K1 Class 2-6-0's allocated to 65J Fort William are stabled side by side next to the turntable – these being Nos 62031 and 62034 as seen on 26th June 1959. Upon closure of the shed to steam early in 1963 two of their number – 62011 and 62012 were transferred but 62031 and 62034 along with 62052 were condemned. (A. N. H. Glover)

177) Rivals at Aberdeen. Ex. North British Railway D34 'Glen' Class 4-4-0 No 62482 *Glen Mamie*, its safety valves roaring, has almost buffered up to ex. Caledonian Railway Class 3F 0-6-0T No 56240, as it waits for a path through the congested station area with a local goods train on 11th August 1953. (Peter Hay)